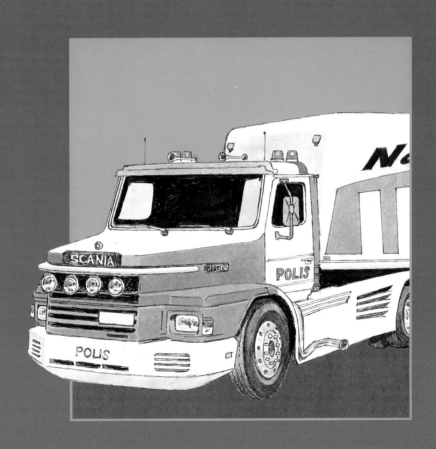

SERIES EDITOR   DAVID SALARIYA
BOOK EDITOR   APRIL McCROSKIE

First published in 1995
by Franklin Watts
a division of the Watts Publishing Group Ltd
96 Leonard Street
London EC2A 4XD

This edition published 2001

ISBN 0 7496 4262 9

Dewey Classification 629.224

Additional artists: Mark Bergin p10-11, John James p10-11

Printed in Belgium

A CIP catalogue record for this book is available from the British Library.

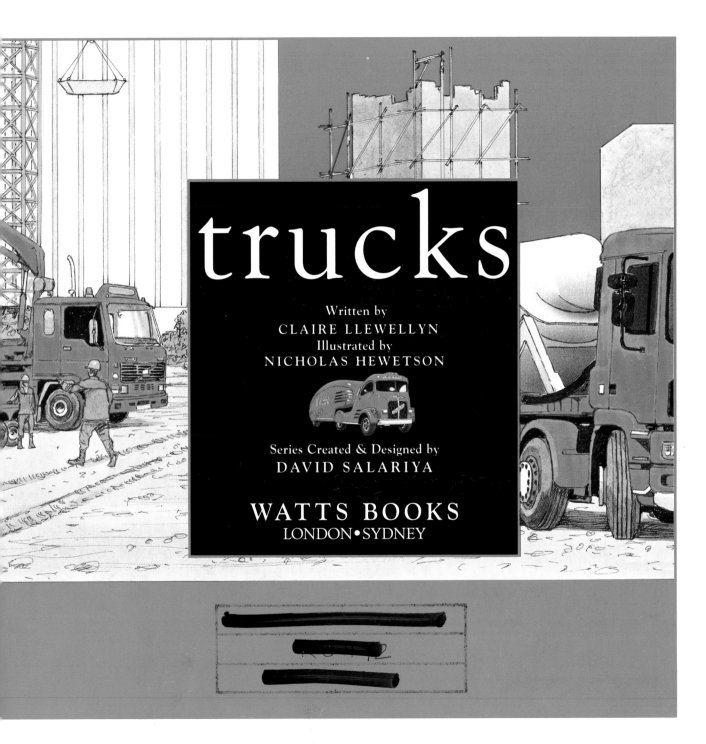

trucks

Written by
CLAIRE LLEWELLYN
Illustrated by
NICHOLAS HEWETSON

Series Created & Designed by
DAVID SALARIYA

WATTS BOOKS
LONDON•SYDNEY

CONTENTS

Introduction	7
What is a Truck?	8
Early Trucks	10
How Trucks Were Used	12
At the Fairground	14
Circus!	16
Trucks in Wartime	18
Today's Trucks	20
In the Driving Seat	22
The Cab	24
Fire Engines	26
At the Building Site	28
Heavy Loads	30
Ambulances	32
Record Breakers	34
Trucks Around the World	36
Useful Words	38
Index	39

Trucks rumble down our roads both day and night. They have been given an important job to do, transporting goods from one end of the country to the other – from ports to factories, from factories to shops, and from shops to our homes.

Since their first appearance over 100 years ago, trucks have changed their engines and design, and now do much more than deliver goods. They work on building sites, keep our streets clean, and provide emergency services at moments of life and death.

Tanker

Flatbed trailer

A liquid load, such as milk, petrol or wine is carried in a long tube-shaped tank. Trucks like these are called tankers.

A truck is a motor vehicle that carries goods from one place to another. It can be anything from a small pick-up truck to a thundering juggernaut. A truck's size, weight, and design all depend on the job it does – from carrying groceries to transporting rock from a quarry.

Trucks are used to shift loads around the farm. These flatbed trailers are stacked with hay.

We see delivery trucks every day of the year, transporting goods all over the country. They manage to get to shops in the most remote places.

A logging truck is both heavy and powerful. It carries tree trunks down from forest plantations.

Logging truck

Delivery truck

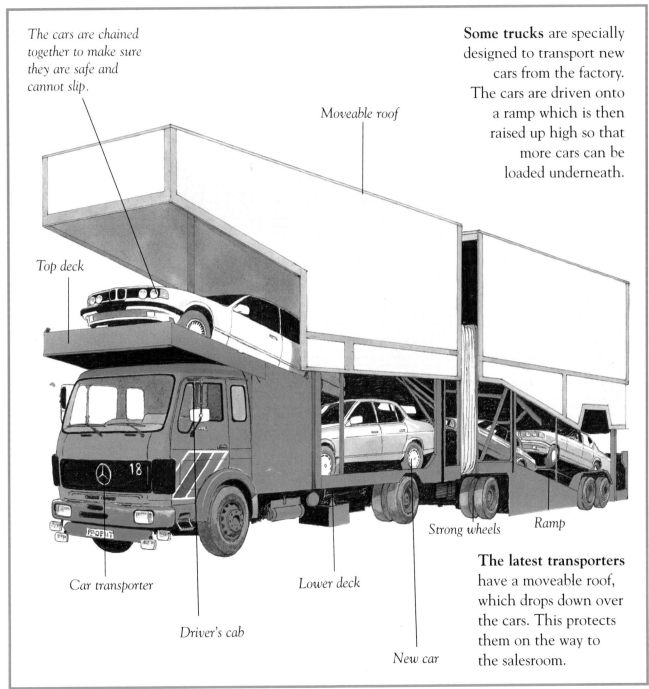

The cars are chained together to make sure they are safe and cannot slip.

Moveable roof

Some trucks are specially designed to transport new cars from the factory. The cars are driven onto a ramp which is then raised up high so that more cars can be loaded underneath.

Top deck

Car transporter

Driver's cab

Lower deck

Strong wheels

Ramp

New car

The latest transporters have a moveable roof, which drops down over the cars. This protects them on the way to the salesroom.

This 16-seat steam coach was built in 1830. It travelled at over 20kph, but had no brakes. The steam engine would cool off and the coach would slow down.

About 200 years ago, the only way to travel or carry goods was behind a gently plodding horse. In the early 1800s, carriages began to appear that were powered by steam engines. These heavy, smoky vehicles were never very popular. As soon as petrol engines were invented, bringing in faster, lighter vehicles, the old steam carriages began to disappear.

In the early 1900s, most goods were transported by rail. To deliver goods to the doorstep, the railway company still relied on a horse and cart.

Ox-drawn wagon

The American pioneers' ox-drawn wagon was a distant ancestor of today's truck.

This German van had a diesel engine. Diesel engines use less fuel than petrol engines and are cheaper to run.

Towards the end of the 1800s, many delivery trucks still ran on steam, like this old mail van.

The French engineer, Nicolas Cugnot, invented the first steam carriage in 1769. It was used by the army to pull heavy cannon.

Cugnot's steam carriage

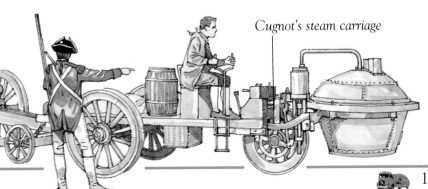

The first trucks

replaced horse-drawn carriages as a way for people to get around. But they were soon used as ambulances, fire engines, road sweepers and even funeral carriages. Trucks also delivered goods, of course – not only in towns, but from one end of the country to the other.

To keep up with the growing number of trucks, better roads were built, and these helped to cut down journey times. But trains still delivered most goods – and did so until the late 1950s.

The development of the horseless carriage began in the mid-1800s.

London's first petrol-engine buses appeared around 1900.

Long-distance truck drivers slept in a bed on top of the cab.

To avoid punctures, trucks had extra wheels and axles to spread the weight.

Diesel truck

By the 1930s, steam engines were being replaced by new diesel trucks. Diesel oil was cheap and went a very long way.

This snowplough was built in about 1920. It was a truck with studded wheels that stopped it getting stuck in the snow.

Studded wheels

This handsome six-wheeled delivery truck belonged to a brewery in Canada during the 1940s.

New air-filled tyres gave drivers a more comfortable ride.

Air-filled tyres

13

Travelling showpeople have always
had to move heavy equipment from one fairground to
another. In the late 1800s, steam-powered traction
engines appeared. 'Traction' means being able to pull
a heavy load. These traction engines could not
only pull the heavy wagons, but could
generate the power to drive the rides.

Traction engines were strong and reliable, and they looked good, too. Many of them were decorated with gleaming brass and colourful paintwork. They caused great excitement when they pulled into town.

These marvellous traction engines were still being used in the 1950s. Turn the page to see a 1950s circus.

The army bought up lots of ordinary trucks in wartime. This one became a tank transporter in World War II (1939-1945).

In wartime, good transport is very important. Tanks and guns, soldiers and supplies are always on the move. During World War I (1914-1918) the armies ordered thousands of trucks. But many of them needed constant repairs, or got stuck in mud.

This truck was once a London bus. During World War I it had the job of transporting carrier pigeons. The birds took important messages from army headquarters to troop leaders.

Modern war trucks have a demanding job to do.

This amphibious truck was used in the 1940s.

Amphibious trucks have tracks which can drive across water or over land.

During air battles, fuel tankers stood by to refuel the returning planes. This was risky as enemy aircraft could strike at any time.

Solving these early problems helped to make better trucks in the future. Military trucks have special needs. As well as being strong, tough and reliable, they need to be high off the ground. This allows them to keep going over muddy ground, and even through streams and rivers.

Modern war vehicles are made from very tough materials. This protects soldiers from powerful modern war weapons.

Fuel tanker

Trucks have come a long way from the slow, draughty vehicles of 100 years ago. Today's supertrucks are comfortable and reliable, and can cruise at high speed for many hours. A truck carries such heavy loads that its chassis has to be strong and heavy, too. All this extra weight needs a more powerful engine to pull it – about four times more powerful than a car's – and equally powerful brakes.

Tread

A truck may have as many as 24 wheels. The grooves on the tyres are called the tread, and help the truck to grip the road.

Trucks like this are called articulated trucks, and can turn corners tightly.

TODAY'S TRUCKS

Tractor unit

Trailer

Trucks are only allowed to carry a certain weight. The lighter the trailer, the heavier the load a truck can carry.

The front of the truck is the tractor unit, with the engine and the driver's cab. On the back is the long trailer that carries the load.

Most cars have five forward gears but a truck may have as many as twenty.

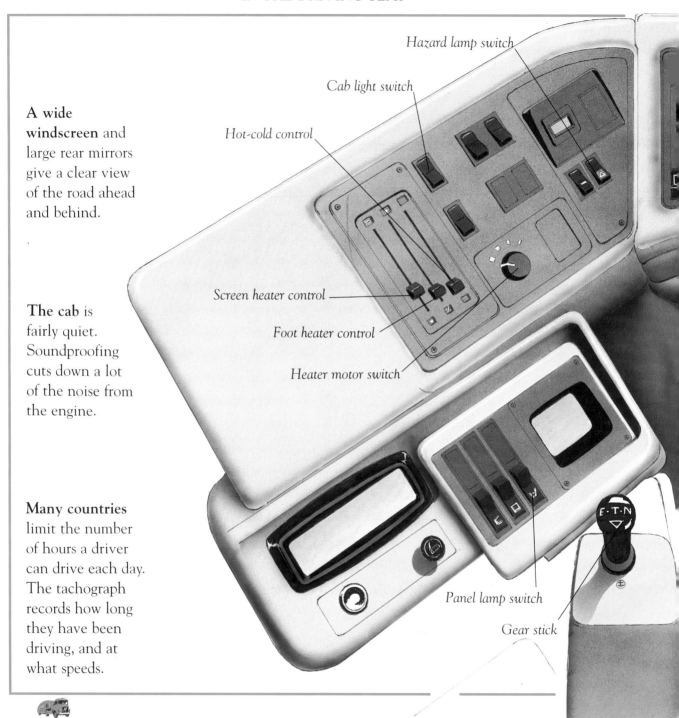

Hazard lamp switch

Cab light switch

Hot-cold control

A wide windscreen and large rear mirrors give a clear view of the road ahead and behind.

Screen heater control

The cab is fairly quiet. Soundproofing cuts down a lot of the noise from the engine.

Foot heater control

Heater motor switch

Many countries limit the number of hours a driver can drive each day. The tachograph records how long they have been driving, and at what speeds.

Panel lamp switch

Gear stick

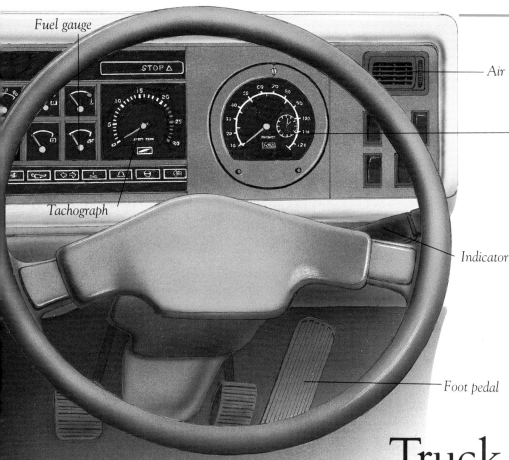

Fuel gauge

STOP △

Air vent to let in fresh air

Speedometer

Tachograph

Indicator

Some cabs look like holiday motor homes, with a sink and cooker as well as a bed. These add comfort for long journeys.

You will see a sleeping compartment if you turn to pages 24 and 25.

Foot pedal

Truck drivers

need to be alert and comfortable. Their seat is cushioned and their cab is light and roomy. On the dashboard there are all sorts of gadgets and instruments to help them. Turn the page to see some very special cab features.

— *Boom*

A long boom carries fire-fighters high into the air, so that they can rescue people from the top of a building.

A fire engine races along the street with its siren blaring as soon as a fire is reported. Fire engines are fast-moving trucks that carry a lot of equipment – tools, ladders, lights, oxygen tanks and so on. Some of them even carry a large water tank, which pumps out water with a terrific force.

Ladders

Hoses

Simba

At an airport fire, the Simba fire engine sprays foam over a burning plane.

Fire engines have to react quickly. They leave within minutes of a call, and reach speeds of 160kph.

Storage compartment

Exhaust

Siren

Light

This fire engine belongs to the American Fire Department.

Dump truck

A mobile crane is a truck with a crane on its back. It has 'legs' to keep the truck steady as the crane is raised.

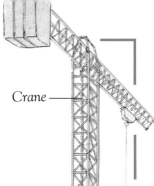

Crane

Dump trucks deliver sand, gravel and cement. Each truck can carry a load that is twice its own weight.

Some trucks are too big to go on the roads. They are brought to the site on the back of huge transporters.

Truck transporter

The cement truck delivers ready-made concrete to the building site. It is mixed inside the drum as the truck moves along.

MAN

Dump trucks are easy to unload. Their body tips back until the load slides out in a heap on the ground.

Trucks do much of the heavy work at a building site. As trenches and holes are dug, hard-working dump trucks carry away the soil and rubble. When building work begins, a fleet of trucks speeds to and fro, bringing load after load of building materials.

Other trucks, such as the cement mixer or crane truck, carry special equipment that is used at the building site itself.

Concrete is mixed inside the drum.

Cement truck

Dump truck

Every truck is designed to carry a load. Most loads are heavy, but some are truly enormous, weighing many hundreds of tonnes. A weight like this would snap the axles of lighter vehicles, but the strongest trucks have a dozen axles, and as many as fifty wheels. These help to spread the weight over the whole truck.

Big trucks drive slowly, and take up a lot of room on the road. They often have a police escort, which helps to warn other drivers.

The first US space shuttle was carried to the launch pad on a huge truck called a crawler. It had caterpillar tracks instead of tyres.

The Dart truck is used in Mexico to carry salt. It is massive, and can carry a load of over 350 tonnes on its journey from the salt mine to the port.

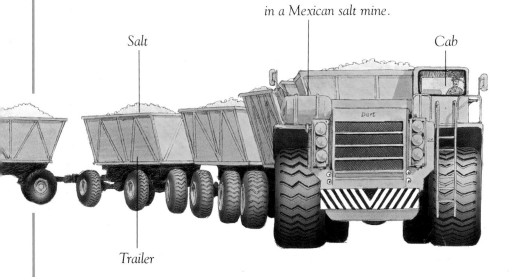

Dart truck at work in a Mexican salt mine.

Salt

Cab

Trailer

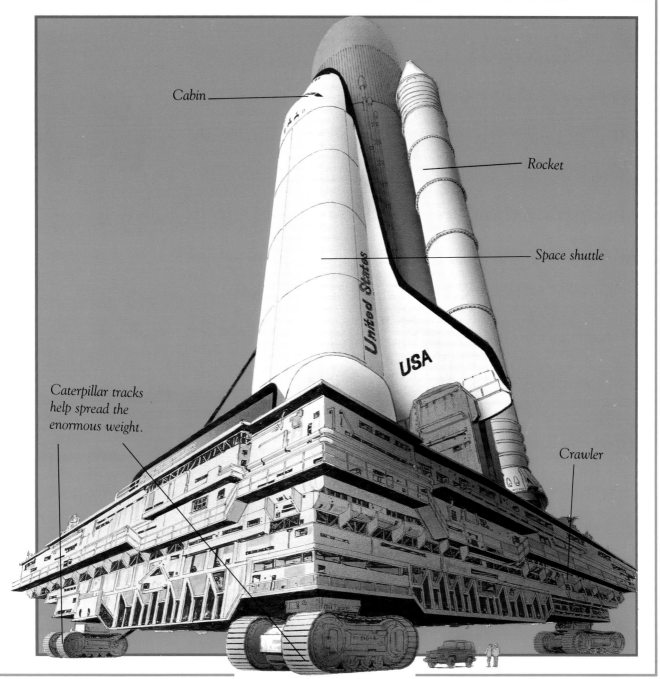

Cabin

Rocket

Space shuttle

Caterpillar tracks
help spread the
enormous weight.

Crawler

USA

United States

Ambulances are fast, powerful trucks that are specially built to deal with emergencies. Every day, trained ambulance crews rush to sick and injured people, give emergency treatment, and then rush them back to hospital. Ambulances give a smooth, comfortable ride, sparing their passengers any painful bumps.

The equipment stored on board may help to keep some patients alive until they can have full medical care.

In the early 1900s, accidents doubled because of the new motor car. An ambulance service was started up with vehicles like this.

It is important to the scene of an accident quickly. Ambulance drivers are trained to drive fast but safely.

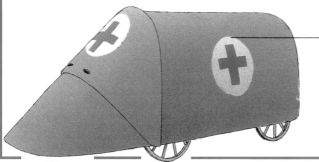

This unusual vehicle was used during World War I. It was a bulletproof stretcher-on-wheels that carried wounded soldiers to safety.

A wailing siren and flashing light warn other road users to get out of the way.

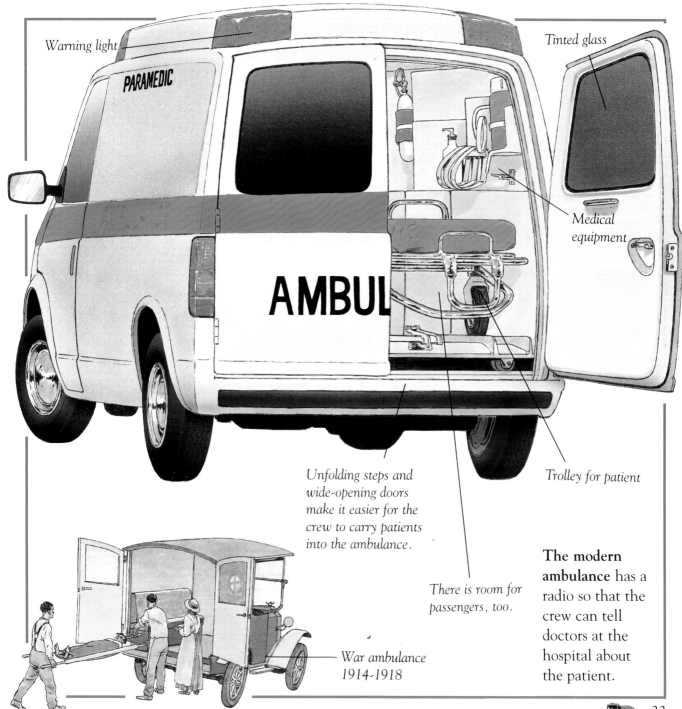

Warning light

PARAMEDIC

Tinted glass

Medical equipment

AMBUL

Unfolding steps and wide-opening doors make it easier for the crew to carry patients into the ambulance.

Trolley for patient

There is room for passengers, too.

War ambulance 1914-1918

The modern ambulance has a radio so that the crew can tell doctors at the hospital about the patient.

The fastest, the slowest, the biggest, the smallest – the world of trucks has its own record breakers. These are not trucks that you see every day on the roads. You may not have seen any of them before. These record breakers have all been specially designed to do a particular job in a particular place – that is what makes them remarkable.

The fastest truck in the world is called ShockWave. Instead of the usual diesel engine, it has three jet engines, which are normally used on a plane. No wonder it can move at over 600kph.

Terex Titan

ShockWave

The Terex Titan is the world's biggest dump truck. Its driver can just reach the bottom rung of the ladder up to the cab.

This truck moves up and down the rows of a Brazilian coffee plantation, picking ripe fruits from the coffee plants. It was the first truck in the world to do this job successfully.

The flattest trucks are the 'tugs' that tow planes around an airport. They are low and flat so that they can zip under a plane's wings.

This little dumper is more like a wheelbarrow than a truck. It carries about 1.5 tonnes and must be one of the smallest trucks in the world.

Airport tug

Trucks are one of the most successful forms of road transport. They are so strong and tough that they can reach small villages that are many days' drive from the nearest railway. This is why trucks are now used in every part of the world. The design of a truck, and the job it does, will often change from one place to another – whether it is in the forests of Canada, the grasslands of Africa, or the burning Australian Outback.

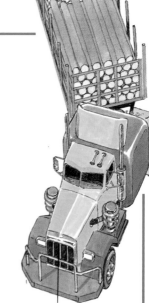

Logging truck

The forests of Canada produce many tonnes of timber. The giant logs are carried to the sawmill on huge trucks.

In Africa, safari trucks are a safe way to look for the animals. They provide a useful viewing platform, too.

Safari truck

Road train

Drivers decorate their buses with special designs and messages that may bring them luck on the roads.

Australian road trains transport goods in places where there are no railways. The tractor pulls three or more trailers.

A bus in Pakistan

Buses in Pakistan are heavy trucks that can cope with the hills.

Narkòtika & Trafik...

INFO

POLIS

SCANIA

POLIS

This Swedish truck is really a police car. It visits schools with information about road safety.

USEFUL WORDS

Amphibious truck
Truck that can move in water as well as over land.

Articulated truck
Truck that is built in two parts.

Axle Metal rod with wheels on each end. Wheels turn on the axle.

Caterpillar tracks
Chains of metal plates, which are used on wheels instead of tyres to spread the weight of the truck, and give grip on rough, muddy ground.

Chassis The body and working parts of a truck are built onto the chassis. It is a strong framework.

Diesel engine
Type of engine used in most trucks. It burns a thick, heavy fuel called diesel, which is made from oil.

Gear Machinery inside a truck that allows the driver to control the power of the engine and the speed of the vehicle.

Generate To make or produce.

Soundproofing
A way of keeping noise out of the cab – by padding for example.

Tachograph An instrument on a truck that records how long and how fast the truck driver has been driving.

Tanker Truck that is specially built to carry a liquid load.

Traction engine
Heavy, steam-powered road vehicle that was once used to pull heavy loads and generate power.

Tractor unit Front of an articulated truck. Contains the engine and the driver's cab.

Trailer unit
The part of an articulated truck that carries the load, and is pulled by the tractor.

INDEX

airport 27, 35
ambulance 12, 32, 33
amphibious truck 19
army trucks 11, 18, 19
articulated truck 20
axle 13, 30

building site 28, 29
bus 12, 18

cab 12, 20, 21, 22, 23
caterpillar tracks 30
cement mixer 28, 29
chassis 20
circus truck 16, 17
crane truck 28, 29
crawler 30
Cugnot, Nicolas 11

Dart truck 30
dashboard 22, 23
delivery truck 8, 11
diesel engine 11, 13
driver 22, 23
dump truck 28, 29, 35

fairground truck 14, 15
fire engine 12, 26, 27
fuel tanker 19

gears 21

horse-drawn vehicle 11, 12

loads 8, 9, 21, 30, 31
logging truck 8, 36

railway 11, 12, 36, 37

road trains 37

safari truck 36
ShockWave 34
Simba 27
snowplough 13
steam engine 10, 11, 14
supertrucks 20

tanker 8, 19
tachograph 23
Titan 35
traction engine 14, 15
tractor unit 20
trailer 8, 21
transporter 9, 18, 29
tread 20
tug 35
tyre 13, 20

wartime truck 18, 19, 32
wheel 13, 20, 30